WS1015
3.99
AF442935

My Communion Album

This keepsake album belongs to

____

____

____

WHITE STAR PUBLISHERS

This Is Me…

I was born on   in

My name is

I am   years old

I am   feet and   inches tall

my hair is

and my eyes are

I was baptized on

at

The Story of My School Life

I'm a   grade student at

of

My favorite subjects are

I hate

Class Photo

My best friends

My favorite books

My favorite sports

Music I like listening to most

What I want to do when I grow up and why

My First Communion Classmates

Group Photo

How We Prepared for
the Sacrament of First Communion

We attended the Parish of

Our Catechist was

What I learnt

Photo with Our Catechists

The 10 Commandments

I am the Lord your God:

1) You shall have no other God before me.

2) You shall not use the Lord's Name in vain.

3) Remember to keep Sabbath day holy.

4) Honour your father and mother.

5) You shall not commit murder.

6) You shall not commit adultery.

7) You shall not steal.

8) You shall not bear false witness against your neighbor.

9) You shall not covet your neighbor's wife.

10) You shall not covet your neighbor's goods.

The Lord's Prayer

Our Father, who art in Heaven,

hallowed be Your name.

Your kingdom come,

Your will be done,

on Earth as it is in Heaven.

Give us this day our daily bread,

and forgive us our trespasses,

as we forgive those who trespass against us,

and lead us not into temptation,

but deliver us from evil.

Amen.

Why Communion is Important

What it Means

The Symbols of Christianity

The **dove** is a symbol of the Holy Spirit: when Jesus was baptized

by John the Baptist, the Spirit of God descended from heaven

in the form of a dove.

The **rainbow** is a symbol of God's love for humanity.

A rainbow appeared in the sky after the Flood as a token

of the covenant which God made with Noah.

Water is a symbol of purification. It represents both life and death:

through Baptism by immersion we are freed from sin and reborn

as sons of God.

The **cross** is the most important symbol of the Christian faith.

It represents Jesus Christ's absolute sacrifice for humanity and therefore the

revelation of God's great love for mankind.

The **fish** is one of the oldest symbols of Christianity.

The letters of the word "fish" are the initials of the

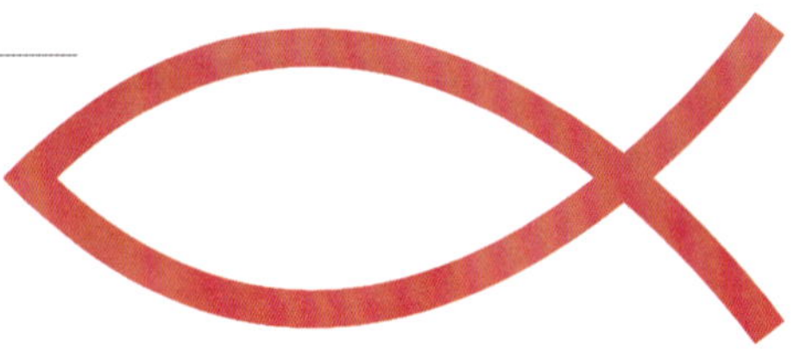

Greek words "Jesus Christ, Son of God, Savior".

The **Chi-Rho** is also one of the most ancient Christian symbols. It is made up

of the Greek letters Chi (χ) and Rho (ρ), the initial letters of the name of Jesus

Christ, and Alpha (α) and Omega (ω), which are the first and last letters of the

Greek alphabet, indicating the presence of Christ from the beginning to the end of time.

Group Photo

My Best Memories of the Catechism Classes

What we did during my Catechism classes

My closest friends were

Why

My Photos

My First Confession

I made my first Confession to Father

How I felt

What the priest said to me

He assigned me the following penances

How I felt afterwards

Act of Contrition

O my God, I am heartily sorry for having offended you,
and I detest all my sins because I dread the loss of heaven
and the pains of hell,
But most of all because they have offended you, my God who are all
good and deserving of all my love.
I firmly resolve, with the help of your grace,
to confess my sins,
to do penance,
and to amend my life.
Amen

Prayer

O Jesus, who loves us so much,

I am sorry for having offended You.

Dear Jesus, with your grace

help me to not offend You again,

because I love You above all things.

Photo

The Day of My First Communion

It was on the

At the   Church

The priest was

How I slept the night before and what I was thinking

My Photos

Taking the Bread...

After taking the cup, He gave thanks and said:
« Take this and divide it among yourselves.
For I say unto you, I will not drink of the fruit of the vine from now on
until the kingdom of God comes ».
And He took the bread, gave thanks and broke it,
and gave it unto them, saying:
« This is My body, given for you: do this in remembrance of Me ».
Likewise, after supper He took the cup, saying:
« This cup is the new testament in my blood, which is shed for you ».
– Jesus –

My Feeling During the Ceremony

What the Priest Recommended We Do During the Ceremony

The Psalms and Hymns he Chose for Us

My Photos

My Resolutions for My Life as a Good Christian

How I Will Put what I Have Learnt into Practice

I Want to Thank God for ...

Dedications and Drawings from My Communion Classmates

Photo of My Family

How My Parents and Family Participated in My First Communion

The person who got the most emotional was

What my mom said to me

What my dad said to me

How my grandparents passed the day with me

My Photo